Exploring God's World with Michael and Caroline Carroll

DINOSAURS!

Michael and Caroline Carroll

Cook Communications

DEDICATION

To our kids, Andy and Allie, who help us explore and appreciate
God's wonderful creation!

ACKNOWLEDGMENTS

The following researchers and visionaries have contributed to the
scientific accuracy of this book:

Robert Bakker, paleontologist, Tate Museum
Kenneth Carpenter, paleontologist, Denver Museum of Natural History
Pastor Duane Cory, Deer Creek Community Church
Celeste Horner, Computer Specialist, Museum of the Rockies
Jack Horner, paleontologist, Museum of the Rockies
Kirk Johnson, paleontologist, Denver Museum of Natural History
Martin Lockley, paleontologist, University of Colorado at Denver
Lorrie McWhinney, Kaiser Permanente
Richard Stucky, Chief Curator, Denver Museum of Natural History
Diana Wiggam, park ranger, Rocky Mountain National Park

COPYRIGHT

PHOTO CREDITS

CONTENTS

MYSTERY MONSTERS

There is a great mystery in our world, a mystery that has puzzled people for a long time. At the edge of the Rocky Mountains, and in the Gobi Desert, and on every continent, we find the bones of creatures who don't live on Earth anymore. Their bones and skin and eggs have *fossilized*, or turned to stone over many years. What were these animals like? What happened to them? What do they tell us about our world, ourselves, and our great God?

The Bible tells us that we can understand things about God by looking at His Creation around us. God's Creation does not lie. Dinosaurs are part of God's Creation. Like all other things in nature, they point toward God and tell us how awesome He is. But even with the information we have discovered we can't solve this riddle: What happened to all the mighty beasts that thundered around on the Earth sometime in the past?

We are unsure about what the dinosaurs and other ancient creatures were really like. Did the movie *Jurassic Park* get it right? Did *Velociraptors* hunt in packs? Did *Tyrannosaurus rex* sniff the air, looking for his next breakfast?

We wonder how long ago dinosaurs lived. Did Noah put dinosaurs on his ark, or were they gone before Noah? Did Job see a dinosaur and call it "behemoth"? Were dinosaurs giant, sluggish lizards who spent time in lakes because they were too heavy to walk around on the land? Or maybe they were lively and fast, jumping and dashing through landscapes of giant ferns and weird plants.

Whatever the answers to our questions, we can be sure that the dinosaurs were magnificent creatures. Some were huge, and some were the size of dogs and cats. Some were quick and some were slow. Some were gentle, some were fierce, and all brought glory to their Creator. Let's explore the world of the dinosaurs!

---

fUN fACTS

Which dinosaur was the hugest? The hugest dinosaur ever found (as of the writing of this book!) is *Argentinosaurus*, about 130 feet long, 80–100 metric tons, closely followed by *Ultrasaurus*, 26 feet tall at the shoulder, 100 feet long, weighing 130 tons.

EARLY DINOSAUR DISCOVERERS
A REAL INDIANA JONES

It was miserably hot. It was windy and sandy. But Roy didn't care. He was used to being in difficult places. And he knew that you have to go to some trouble to find good fossils.

Ever since he had worked as a janitor in New York's American Museum of Natural History, Roy Chapman Andrews had wanted to go to China. The museum sometimes sent Roy off to strip meat from the bones of whales that washed ashore so the skeletons could be brought to the museum. Back at the museum, when he wasn't scrubbing floors, stuffing birds, and polishing tables, Roy spent his time looking at the fossil collections and dreaming of distant lands. Many of the fascinating creatures came from China. He decided he wanted to go there someday.

At last, in 1922, Roy was sent on an expedition to the Gobi Desert at the edge of Mongolia. It was just the kind of adventure he had always dreamed of, and he returned to the desert several years later with more scientists who shared his excitement about finding ancient life in the rocks. Roy was a hero to many, leading explorers on great adventures into dangerous and exotic places. He fought off bandits with guns. He hiked across high cliffs and climbed down deep canyons.

The greatest discovery came when Roy's expedition got lost in Mongolia. Roy stopped to ask for directions. As he spoke with a wrinkled frontier soldier, his photographer friend went exploring. J. B. Shackleford walked away from the expedition's cars and camels to get a good look at a distant volcano and nearly tumbled over a cliff! Shackleford had found a deep chasm of orange walls and spires called the "Flaming Cliffs." After one look at the bones poking out of the cliff, Roy knew this was an important place.

The explorers found one dinosaur with a skull about seven inches long, bristling with sharp teeth. It had a flat claw like an eagle. Its big head meant that it was probably smart, and there were places in its skull for large, hunter's eyes. Roy's expedition named this lean and mean killer *Velociraptor*.

The Flaming Cliffs also held the fossils of dinosaur eggs. Until Roy's expedition, nobody knew that dinosaurs laid eggs. In fact, some scientists thought the eggs were from an extinct bird instead of a dinosaur. Today, scientists have found many kinds of dinosaur eggs, some with fossilized babies inside. And much of what we have learned is because of an adventurous man who started out as a janitor but became one of the world's most famous paleontologists! Adventurers like Roy Chapman Andrews provided inspiration for the movie character Indiana Jones.

Roy and his friends were not the first people to see dinosaur fossils. Many legends of dragons and giants were probably inspired by huge dinosaur bones found in the countryside. The ancient Greeks told of a creature called a griffin, half bird and half lion. Griffins were said to live in the Altai mountains of Mongolia, where they guarded secret treasures. They had four legs, wings on their shoulders, a strong bird-beak, and a horn on top of their head. Guess what is just south of the Altai mountains? The Gobi Desert, where Roy and others found many dinosaur fossils. One of the most common fossils found there is from a creature called *Protoceratops*. This dinosaur walked on four legs, had a large beak, and had a long shoulder blade. His skull looked like it had a horn on top, although it was really a shield, as we will see in our "Prehistoric Portraits" section. Fossils of *Protoceratops* could have easily inspired the legend of the griffin (See page 11).

One of the earliest dinosaur discoverers was an English woman named Mary Ann Mantell. She loved looking at rocks, and so did her husband, a doctor. One day in 1822, while her husband was treating one of his patients, Mary Ann went for a walk outside the patient's country house. As Mary Ann looked at some wildflowers, she noticed a pile of rocks dumped by the road. In some of those rocks were shiny, fossilized teeth. Mary Ann Mantell had discovered the first evidence of the dinosaur *Iguanodon*. She and her husband decided to track down where the rocks came from. They finally ended up at a rock quarry, where many more fossils were waiting for them. Dr. Mantell called fossils "medallions of Creation." There is a lesson here: Keep your eyes open and always notice the rocks!

Roy Chapman Andrews

Soon everyone wanted to become a dinosaur hunter. Othniel Marsh and Edward Cope were famous for their race to get the most fossils. In their rush to get the "biggest and best," much science was lost. But people like them made dinosaurs very popular. As more dinosaurs were found, people assumed that the creatures were like giant lizards because of the shapes of their skeletons. Sir Richard Owen, who later started the British Museum, noticed that the bones of *Megalosaurus* and *Iguanodon* were different from any living lizard. In 1842, to describe our fossilized friends, he came up with the name **dinosaur**, or "terrible lizard." It's a great name, but not very accurate, as we will see later.

As people dug up more and more fossils, they began to realize that these creatures were different at different layers of the Earth. They finally figured out, just as scientists who studied old cities knew, that different layers of rock were from different periods of time. Scientists have given names to the three periods of time when dinosaurs lived. **Triassic** fossils are in the deepest and oldest layers of rock. **Jurassic** fossils come next. And the **Cretaceous** fossils are in the top layers, because they come from the most recent dinosaurs. Labeling layers from oldest to newest helps the field researchers know not only *where* they are digging for fossils, but also *when* they are digging for fossils.

The time scale used by scientists today was given to us by several Christian preachers in the 1800s. One was the Reverend William Buckland, a conservative Anglican preacher in England. Buckland enjoyed what he called "God's steps of Creation." In fact, Buckland's horse was so used to stopping at interesting layered rock that when Buckland fell asleep in the saddle, the horse would stop at a rocky outcrop and snort to wake him. Like many Christians before him, Buckland believed that Creation was "written in many acts and scenes."

A PREACHER MEETS THE DINOSAURS

Edward Hitchcock was a busy guy. He was a pastor who preached every Sunday to a very conservative congregation in New England. He was a professor at Amherst College. And if that wasn't enough, he was the state **geologist** (rock expert) for Massachusetts. Hitchcock was the first person to identify the ancient creatures that Sir Richard Owen would name "dinosaurs."

Hitchcock was one of the most famous and respected American geologists of the 1800s. His dinosaur work was based mostly on footprints. Hitchcock realized that the footprints found in the New England stone were left by animals different from anything known. He called the dinosaurs a "race of flightless birds of gigantic size." Hitchcock described these creatures as having claws on their arms instead of wings. This is an almost perfect description of a *Velociraptor* or a tyrannosaur.

Hitchcock taught his students at Amherst College how to go out into the mission field and preach the gospel. He also encouraged them to send him back fossils from wherever they traveled. He put together what is still the largest collection of fossil footprints in the world.

Every Sunday, Hitchcock brought geology into his sermons. He told his congregation that God's truths were to be found in the Bible and in His Creation, as the book of Romans tells us. "For since the creation of the world God's invisible qualities—his eternal power and divine nature—have been clearly seen, being understood from what has been made . . ." (Romans 1:20). Hitchcock showed us that the world has recorded history in the rocks and that the world's history has unfolded over a long period of time. After all, he pointed out, Genesis shows God creating the universe in steps over a period of time and that God did not "cease creating" until he made Adam and Eve. Edward Hitchcock helped people to see that the awesome power and majesty of God are echoed in the fossils, rocks, and mountains around us.

(Above) Sketch of dinosaur footprints done by Reverend Hitchcock

(Opposite) The legend of the mythical griffin (at right) may have been inspired by the fossilized remains of the dinosaur *Protoceratops*, at left (painting after work by Adrian Mayor and Celeste Horner).

(Top) These dinosaur tracks in Morrison, Colorado, are a kind of imprint fossil. The wide footprints were left behind by large herbivores. Smaller, three-toed prints that look like chicken feet were made by the feet of carnivores, perhaps following the herbivores for their next meal!

(Bottom) Skull of a *Protoceratops* like the ones found by Andrews' expedition. Notice the beak on the front of the skull and the frill on the back.

HOW FOSSILS ARE FORMED

Fossils are the remains of living things that have **petrified**, or turned to stone. Today, the only traces left of the mighty dinosaurs are these fossils of their bones, eggs, teeth, skin, feathers, footprints, and droppings. It takes a long time to make a fossil. An animal dies and is buried under sand or mud. The soft parts usually rot away, but the hard parts, like bones and teeth, remain. Over many years, more mud and sand settle on top, slowly turning into rock. Water carrying minerals seeps into the rock, and the minerals soak into the dead ani-

mal's bones. The minerals replace the bones with hard rock. Sometimes dinosaur bones are more bone than rock. The bone material remains, but the little holes and veins in the bone are filled with minerals, so the bone is a mix of the original material and rock.

There are some other ways that fossils are made. One is called an **imprint fossil**. A dinosaur may walk across a muddy beach, leaving its footprints. The footprints dry out and are filled in with sand, then slowly turn to rock. Another kind of fossil is formed when the skeleton in the rock is completely dissolved by minerals, leaving an empty space in the shape of the creature. This is called a **natural mold**. The paleontologist can pour **resin** or **plaster** into this natural mold to make a perfect copy of the skeleton.

A lot can happen to mix up a dead animal's remains before they are fossilized. When an animal dies, **scavengers**—animals that feed on dead things—usually come around and eat the meat, and the bones get scattered around. Sometimes dead creatures are washed down rivers, where they collect in a pile on an island or at a bend in the river. This big pile of bones is like a giant jigsaw puzzle for the paleontologists, and many years are spent figuring out which bones belong to which beast. It's amazing that we have ever found a complete dinosaur skeleton!

SOME NEW FOSSIL FINDS

Fortunately, some big **fossil fields** have been found with many creatures all in one piece and all in one place. One of the best fossil fields is at a site called the Burgess Shale in Canada. The fossils of ancient sea creatures here are very well preserved. Scientists think that an undersea

The weird and wonderful creatures of the Burgess Shale were preserved beneath an underwater landslide.

Key:
1. Eldonia
2. Anomalocaris
3. Sidneyia
4. Dinomischus
5. Marella
6. Wiwaxia
7. Aysheaia
8. Ottoia worm
9. Hallucigenia worm

landslide buried these critters. In the Gobi Desert of Mongolia, there has been the exciting new find of a complete *Oviraptor.* This dinosaur died on its nest of twenty or more eggs, probably trying to protect them. It was most likely buried by a sandstorm or a collapsing sand cliff.

It is difficult to guess what dinosaurs looked like just from their bones. There is no color left in fossils, and usually there is no soft part of the body left. But sometimes God leaves us more clues. In some places, dinosaur skin has been found. Dinosaur skin is scaly, and some of it looks knobby or bony. In northeastern China a three-foot-long dinosaur from the early Cretaceous period has been

found with feathers! Its tiny feathers run along the edge of the fossil from the top of its head all the way down to the tip of its tail. These feathers look like the down found on the underside of ducks. This is exciting news for paleontologists, many of whom are working to find out if dinosaurs were more like birds than reptiles.

Another bit of dino evidence comes from Italy. Within limestone there, rock hunters found a nine-inch-long dinosaur which was nearly complete. It was missing only part of its tail and the lower half of its legs. This little cousin of *Velociraptor* had fossilized intestines, a fossilized liver, and fossilized muscles in its long neck.

THE STRANGE CASE OF THE SICK STEGOSAURUS

The bones of a dinosaur have many stories to tell. It takes a creative scientist to understand just what a dinosaur's skeleton can tell us. Take the example of a *Stegosaurus* found in Colorado.

Paleontologist Kenneth Carpenter of the Denver Museum of Natural History had a problem. He was studying the newly discovered skeleton of a *Stegosaurus* when he noticed something strange about her tail. Bruce Rothschild, another paleontologist who studies sickness in ancient creatures, suggested that this *Stegosaurus* had died of an infection in one of her tail spikes.

Ken turned the project over to Lorrie McWhinney, one of his volunteers, who was interested in ancient disease. Lorrie had access to a special kind of x-ray machine called a **CAT scan** (Computerized Axial Tomography). Lorrie took images of the dinosaur's bony tail section. She found evidence that the bone had become infected when the tip of the tail spike had broken off. Small holes in the bone showed places where pus had come out and bumpy areas where the bone had swelled.

Of the fifty Stegosaur tail spikes found in the world, four have been broken. It is no wonder: Stegosaurs used their tails as weapons, swinging the spikes at their attackers. In the case of Ken and Lorrie's dinosaur, the *Stegosaurus*' tail spike may have broken when she was fighting off a nasty **carnivore** (meat-eater), or she may have broken it in an accident. The bone developed **osteomyelitis**, a bone infection, which was so bad that it spread to another spike. People get osteomyelitis too. It is serious, but it can be treated with antibiotics. But there were no dino-doctors around for this *Stegosaurus*. Eventually, she became too sick to take care of herself.

Dr. Carpenter believes the *Stegosaurus*, already sick from her bone infection, may have waded into a waterhole to cool off when she died. Her forelegs and shoulder blades were never found, and there were teeth marks on some of her bones. Carpenter believes scavengers carried off parts of the dinosaur. Fortunately for us, they left most of this animal behind.

Whatever happened in the end, this sick *Stegosaurus* has taught us much about dinosaurs of her kind.

(Top) The *Stegosaurus* used her tail to fight off predators like the mighty *Allosaurus*. *Allosaurus* bones have been found with gashes and splits that might have come from a meeting like this one. Notice how *Stegosaurus'* plates overlapped on her neck but became one row on her back and tail. These plates gave her added protection. (Bottom Left) Lorrie McWhinney holds the tail spike of a *Stegosaurus*. Lorrie studied the spike using medical technology. (Bottom Right) This *Stegosaurus* tail spike shows signs of infection sometime during the creature's life.

Tyrannosaurus rex scares Troödons away from a meal.
(Inset Left) The teeth of a *Tyrannosaurus rex*.
(Inset Right) A paleontologist holds up the claw of a fierce
Velociraptor next to the giant claw of a tyrannosaur.

THE HUNTERS

The most scary and exciting of all the dinosaurs are the carnivores, or meat-eaters. Meat-eating dinosaurs are called **theropods**. Theropods walked on their hind legs and had grasping arms with two or three clawed fingers on each hand. Scientists believe that many of the theropods were quite intelligent, because they had fairly large brains compared with other creatures.

Tracks in Massachusetts and British Columbia show that some small meat-eaters hunted in groups. Packs of small, sharp-toothed meat-eaters must have been a scary sight. A small *Coelophysis*, *Dilophosaurus,* or *Velociraptor* was savage enough with its sharp teeth and fast movements. But larger dinosaurs would have had a hard time getting away from many hunting together. Large members of the tyrannosaur family like *Albertosaurus* and *Daspletosaurus* probably hunted alone or

(Top) Some scientists believe *T-rex* hunted other dinosaurs, like these duck-billed hadrosaurs. Fossils of tyrannosaurs have been found in Alaska, where the beasts would have hunted under the northern lights.
(Top Right) Theropods, or meat-eating dinosaurs, had bird-like feet with claws.
(Bottom Left & Right) T-rex had huge chompers. Some of his teeth were eight inches long! But what did he eat with them?

in pairs. They had heavy skulls and may have attacked by running head-first into their prey with their jaws open, knocking over their dino-meal with their toothy heads. Tyrannosaurs, allosaurs, and *Velociraptors* seem like the monsters of nightmares, but they were very important for keeping a natural balance in the **ecosystem**. Like lions, cougars, and other carnivores today, the animals they ate were usually the weak or the sick. This left the healthiest animals to continue on. The meat-eaters, like the plant-eaters, were an important part of God's design for life on Earth.

T-REX: PREDATOR OR SCAVENGER?

The most famous of the big carnivores is *Tyrannosaurus rex*. Its name means "Tyrant King of the Lizards." From the front of its nose to the tip of its tail, this Cretaceous terror stretched 50 feet and towered 20 feet high. An adult human would barely reach to *T-rex's* knees! But was *T-rex* a hunter-predator or a scavenger? Because of the shape of its teeth and its tiny front legs, paleontologist Jack Horner believes that *T-rex* was a scavenger—probably the most successful scavenger of the time. *T-rex* teeth are banana-shaped, not knife-like, which makes them good for crushing the bones of dead animals to get nutrients. *T-rex* legs were not spread apart for running or chasing, and its eyes were small compared with known hunters.

To those of us who feel let down about this, Dr. Horner says: "What's so honorable about killing? Scavenging is a very efficient way to get fed. There are no predators who do any better than catching one

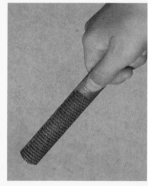

(Top) The skull and neck of a hadrosaur.
Note the bent, buffalo-like neck and the "duck bill" area around the mouth.
(Bottom Left) The duck-billed hadrosaurs had teeth arranged in rows, like this file, to eat tough plants.
(Bottom Right) Hadrosaurs had feet shaped like hooves.

out of every ten prey animals they go after. They burn a lot of calories to catch one meal. Scavengers . . . can get the food away from the predator with no problem. For example, when a cheetah catches something, it eats as much as it can as quickly as it can, and if a hyena comes, it just chases the cheetah away. The cheetah will not fight for its life over the carcass—it can always catch another one. This same thing probably happened with predators such as *Velociraptor* and *Deinonychus*—*T-rex* was bigger, nastier, and meaner, and he could go in there and kick whoever it was out of the way. Scavenging is the quickest, easiest, safest way to acquire meat." Some paleontologists disagree, pointing to the tail of a hadrosaur with a bite taken out. Only a *T-rex* could have reached up that far. Many believe that *T-rex* was both a scavenger and a hunter. But if Dr. Horner is right, maybe a better name for *T-rex* would be "King of the Garbage-collectors"!

THE HUNTED:
DUCK-BILLED DINOSAURS

Theropods hunted all sorts of dinosaurs, usually **herbivores,** or plant-eaters. One item on the menu must have been the duck-billed dinosaurs. The duckbills came in two types. The hadrosaur duckbills had flat heads, while lambeosaur duckbills had many elegant styles of crests. A duckbill had no obvious way to defend itself, no plates or spikes or bony shields. Its legs were not designed for running fast. Its hoofed toes were spread wide for walking on soft ground or mud, and some scientists believe it may have taken to swimming in rivers or lakes to get away from predators. It had a bill-shaped mouth with sharp edges, a good shape for cropping leaves.

When first discovered, it was thought that the duckbill dinosaur had weak teeth and probably spent its life in swamps and rivers, eating soft water plants with its loose teeth and wide bill. But as better fossil jaws were found, it was discovered that its teeth were arranged in strong rows. In fact, these creatures had hundreds of teeth that worked together like a rasping file. It is now believed that duckbills probably didn't spend a lot of time in water but ate plants found on dry land. Fossilized conifer needles, twigs, and pine seedlings have been found in duckbill stomachs.

When it wasn't avoiding predators, the duckbill spent much of its time grazing. It probably did not rear up to eat tall trees, but stayed close to the ground at meal time, eating like a "walking lawn mower," says Ken Carpenter. The reason for this is the shape of the back: at the shoulders, a duckbill's backbone bends downward. This permanent bend is a lot like a bison's, whose back is bent at the front. A bison keeps his head down, and a duckbill would have done the same. Since its front arms were small, it probably walked on its back legs, using the tail for balance. It may have used the front arms to touch the ground every once in a while when moving, for rooting up things to eat, and for digging nests.

ARMORED DINOSAURS: BRING YOUR PLATE WITH YOU!

Many dinosaurs were designed for protection from predators. **Stegosaurs** had rows of plates sticking up from their backs and a series of spikes on their tails. *Stegosaurus stenops* had four spikes at the end of the tail. *Kentrosaurus* had plates in front, which got thinner and sharper as they moved back toward the tail, where they became spikes.

At the top of the Jurassic layers of stone and moving into the Cretaceous, new armored dinosaurs begin to appear in the fossil record. They are called the **nodosaurs** and include such curious creatures as *Hylaeosaurus, Sauropelta,* and *Nodosaurus.* Unlike the stegosaurs, these creatures had a coat of armored plates covering their entire bodies, with shields, bumps, knobs, and spikes. For a long time, nodosaurs were mysterious; most skeletons found were missing important parts. But very recently, a nearly complete new nodosaur, called *Gastonia,* was found in Utah.

There were thunderstorms in dinosaur times, just as there are today. Here, a pack of *Triceratops* runs from a wildfire started by lightning. Notice their steer-like horns and frilled collars.
(Opposite) *Gargoyleosaurus* with *Rhamphorhynchus* blocking sun.

Nodosaurs were built wide and low like a Humvee. The only soft place on a nodosaur was its belly, and even it was covered with pea-sized pieces of bone. A tyrannosaur would have had a hard time turning it over, and its spikes made the nodosaur dangerous to get near. Perhaps nodosaurs defended themselves by curling up on the ground like armadillos—with their armor protecting them—waiting for their attacker to get bored and go away.

But some scientists think they were far more lively: the shape of their front leg bones show us that they had strong elbows, perfect for lunging or jumping at an attacker. Their shoulder spikes could be used as deadly weapons.

Another group of armored heavies were the **ankylosaurs**. These wonderful creatures had blocky heads with armor on the top and sides. Small teeth along the jaw led to a beak in front. Ankylosaurs probably couldn't move as fast as nodosaurs. To make up for their slowness, they had extra plates protecting their heads, with small horns at the back corners. Their most important weapons, however, were their club-like tails. These truck-sized creatures could swing them fiercely. One of the largest ankylosaurs was *Eoplocephalus*. These knights-in-bony-armor were 20 feet long and may have weighed two tons. Their leathery skin was covered with small bone shields. Rows of spikes went down the center of their backs and tails. Even their eyelids were bony!

Ceratopsians, or horned dinosaurs, were armored with neck frills, beaks, and horns to protect them from enemies. They also could have used these horns to battle for a mate in the same way that deer or rams do. The first to be discovered was *Protoceratops,* the dinosaur found by Roy Chapman Andrews' expedition to Mongolia.

God gave armored dinosaurs shields, clubs, spears, and natural swords long before people invented these things.

FLYING CREATURES:
WINGS WITHOUT FEATHERS

Dinosaurs looking into the prehistoric sky often saw strange creatures of the air. Some were the size of small sparrows, and some spread great wings as far across as a house. They looked much like birds but were actually reptiles. Many of these flying reptiles had fur or hair covering at least part of their bodies. Called **pterodactyls**, or **pterosaurs**, all of them had hollow bones like birds, big heads compared with their bodies, long rear legs, and front arms built like great wings. Their wings were not like bird wings, because they had no feathers. Instead, the wing was a thin sheet of skin like a bat's wing.

Did pterosaurs flap their wings, or did they glide? Paleontologists are not sure. Some pterosaur wings were not shaped for soaring. Creatures like the giant *Quetzalcoatlus*, with a 50-foot wing span,

> **FUN FACTS**
>
> **How many dinosaur species have been found?** Over 600 species have been identified so far. Scientists suspect that hundreds of species of dinosaurs will never be found, because they were very small and bird-like, with delicate bones which were scattered or eaten, leaving no fossil record.

must have had to flap to stay aloft. But other pterosaurs may have been able to float on the wind like eagles. Some had tails shaped like rudders for steering. *Rhamphorhynchus* had a long tail with a diamond-shaped kite on the end. His neck was long like a swan's, and his head was shaped like a spear for catching fish.

Another fascinating flyer was the *Dimorphodon*. Like other creatures of the air, *Dimorphodon* had a graceful, S-shaped neck, so that he could hold his huge head over his body in flight, much like a pelican does. Sharp teeth lined his beak both above and below.

When they weren't flying, pterosaurs had to get around on the ground. How did they do it? Pterosaurs walked on all fours like vampire bats. Many scientists believe that those with long tails used them for balance, much like kangaroos. They must have folded their great wings and hopped or run along the ground. Many pterosaur footprint trackways show impressions where their wing tips were used like

front feet. They could also roost in trees: their claws were similar to those of squirrels, who can scamper up and down trees and even rocky cliffs.

These bizarre flying reptiles seem so alien to us, with their long necks and bat-like wings. But they are a part of God's Creation as much as today's birds of the air and the fish of the seas. The psalmist reminds us that God says, "I know every bird in the mountains, and the creatures of the field are mine." (Psalm 50:11) We have never seen these magnificent creatures alive, but thanks to their fossils we can marvel at how wonderful they were.

SEA-FARING REPTILES: FINS AND TEETH

During the age of the dinosaurs, there were wonderful creatures that dove and swam and danced through the oceans. They were not true dinosaurs, but many were just as big and beautiful. We would even recognize some of them: there were sea turtles and ocean-going crocodiles. But there were stranger—and much larger—creatures, too.

Best known are the **plesiosaurs**, with their long necks and flippers. The plesiosaur *Elasmosaurus* had one of the longest necks in the animal kingdom. Other plesiosaurs had short necks and probably swam like seals.

There were also great swimming creatures called **ichthyosaurs**. Their lizard-like heads were full of sharp teeth and grew on a fish-like body with flippers instead of fins. One kind of ichthyosaur looked like a porpoise, and the largest, *Shonisaurus*, was 50 feet long! These great animals looked like fish but breathed air like reptiles.

Mosasaurs were true lizards. Their hands and feet were shaped like paddles, and their sharp teeth were designed for eating darting fish—which means that they ate fast food!

Another strange creature of the deep was called *Hesperornis*. This bird-swimmer had webbed feet and no wings. It probably paddled with its feet, like water birds such as penguins do today.

DINOSAUR LIFESTYLES

FAMILY LIFE

Scientists believe that some dinosaurs lived in families and were very social creatures. Footprint trackways of duckbills show that the adults spread out in front as the herd traveled, sometimes walking side by side. Young duckbills followed behind, often stepping on their parents' footprints. Other herbivore footprints around tree impressions show us that these dinosaurs fed in groups.

VELOCIRAPTOR

Says paleontologist Robert Bakker, "What's most exciting to me right now is the new information about dinosaur lives—what they would face every day, their family relationships. If you're born a *Velociraptor*, are you on your own? Or are you protected until you are full grown? We have the first well-preserved nest of meat-eating raptors. They dragged food into the nest for their young. There's a thigh bone in one nest from a ten-ton prey animal. On the bones are tiny little scratch marks. The young chewed on it. And dinosaurs, like crocodiles, would break teeth off all the time and new teeth would grow in. So every time a baby chewed on something hard, a tooth or two would break off and new ones would grow in. These broken tooth crowns are markers of who chewed what, where. It's like finding spent bullets at a crime scene. You can tell which species was chewing. We

find baby teeth next to adult teeth— both chewing on the same bone at the same time. So we can prove that the *Velociraptors* provided for their young until they were grown."

MAIASAUR

Paleontologist Jack Horner has discovered an entire nesting ground where thousands of duckbilled maiasaurs may have lived together, caring for their young. In 1978, Horner visited a roadside rock shop, where he came across some rare baby dinosaur bones in a coffee can. The owners took him to the Montana cattle ranch where the bones had been found, and the site turned out to be the first known dinosaur nest! Apparently, the area was the nesting ground for a herd of 10,000 maiasaurs. Their mud nests were located on high ground and surrounded by streams, so that the parents could guard their helpless young from predators.

FUN FACTS

Which is the oldest dinosaur?
The earliest dinosaur found so far is *Eoraptor*, from the Triassic period.

(Opposite) Paleontologists can tell that parent *Velociraptors* brought food to their babies. Large bones with bite marks from both adults and babies have been found.

ORODROMEUS AND TROÖDON

Another site, called Egg Mountain, was the nesting colony of some small herbivores called *Orodromeus*. They laid their eggs on small islands in a lake and guarded them carefully. But once the babies hatched, they were ready to run and were left on their own. The clever, carnivorous *Troödons* laid their own eggs near the *Orodromeus* nests. The *Troödon* hatchlings feasted on any *Orodromeus* eggs or babies that they could get their sharp little teeth on.

DINO DINNERS

Dinosaur diets are somewhat mysterious, because the things dinosaurs ate were almost never fossilized inside of them. But some things are known. Meat eaters probably ate whatever animals they could get their claws on, mostly other dinosaurs, but perhaps some pterosaurs and lizards, too. There is evidence that tyrannosaurs ate both ceratopsians and duckbills. Bite marks have been found on bones of these creatures, and *T-rex* teeth have also been found among their remains.

The long-necked **sauropods** are thought to have eaten tall vegetation. Like giraffes, they may have eaten the tops of trees that shorter dinos couldn't reach. Sauropods prob-

A Maiasaur munches on some "berry good" plants.

ably fed on a variety of plants. Preserved prehistoric food in their stomachs includes conifers, cycads, ferns, and horsetail plants. In some hadrosaur fossils, twigs, berries, and other coarse plant material has been found. Scientists believe they nosed around close to the ground, eating rough plants. The shape of their teeth, much like a file, shows that they were made to eat tough plants.

It boggles the mind to think about how much the sauropods would have needed to eat to nourish their enormous bodies. Scientists estimate that the largest sauropods may have consumed a ton of foliage every day. That would be a pile of ferns, twigs, berries, and pine needles equal to the weight of a car!

Other clues about dino dinners can be found in **coprolites**. Coprolite is just a fancy name for dinosaur droppings. Scientists study this fossilized dung to find out how and what dinosaurs ate. Recent studies of an ancient *Tyrannosaurus* coprolite found jagged bone fragments, proving that instead of swallowing his food whole, like modern reptiles do, *T-rex* chewed first!

JACK HORNER: THE MAN BEHIND JURASSIC PARK

During the filming of *Jurassic Park*, Jack Horner was beside Stephen Spielberg as his consultant. "*Jurassic Park* used dinosaurs as actors," Horner says. "My job was to make sure that *all* the actors looked their part, whether they were dinosaurs or Alan Grant. I also made sure that the actors pronounced their words correctly, so that they would come across as paleontologists, and the sixth graders wouldn't send nasty letters to Stephen Spielberg." In fact, the character of Alan Grant is based on Horner.

In addition to dinosaur acting, Horner has a lot to say about how science is done. "If you're a detective, you work through all the possibilities, and you come up with the most likely one *based on the evidence you have.* Then you look for something that would prove that your conclusion is wrong. You're always looking for something to show that you are wrong. The more tests that you make that don't show that you're wrong, the more likely it is that it's true."

Horner points to the great bone bed of maiasaur nesting sites found in Montana. The **hypothesis** (the idea scientists have) is that all 10,000 dinosaur fossils belong to maiasaurs who lived together there. "We can probably only identify twenty of them as maiasaur. The rest we can tell are duckbills of some kind. Our

(Top) Jack and Celeste Horner
(Middle) Nesting Maiasaur
(Bottom) Fossilized Maiasaur eggs

hypothesis is that they are all maiasaur, and from that we think that they lived together and died together, that they traveled in herds. It all can be falsified with one bone, but that is how you do science." Horner says that other kinds of dinosaurs may have been there, in which case his hypothesis is not true. "There might be some other kinds of dinosaurs there. But 'might be' isn't really science. We must deal in what we see." There is another way of doing science, Horner warns. "If you think you're right about something, and you go around looking for evidence that supports your idea, there's a pretty good chance that you are not going to find things to disprove your idea. You ignore some things that come along. That is not a good way of doing science."

DINOSAUR fASHIONS

When it comes to glamour, the peacock has nothing on the dinosaurs. Dinosaurs sported crests, frills, crowns, spikes, and plates. Many of these exotic dino duds were designed for protection, while other fancy features may have helped them to sing or show off to attract mates.

Dinosaur fashion also may have included bright colors. If dinosaurs were bird-like, then perhaps their colors were like those found in parrots, toucans, and flamingos! Many were undoubtedly colored so that they could hide. This kind of "blending in" coloration is called **camouflage**. Tigers, deer, rabbits, and other animals today have coloration that helps them hide from predators.

We know the stegosaurs used their plates for protection. The plates undoubtedly helped stegosaurs to look big, but they also might have been used to cool off in the breeze, much as an elephant uses its ears to keep cool on hot days.

Ceratopsian headgear was spectacular. One of the most famous ceratopsians is *Triceratops*, with its magnificent triple horns. *Monoclonius* had one prominent horn, while creatures like *Styracosaurus* had many. **Pachycephalosaurs** ("thick-headed reptiles") are rarely found in the fossil record. These strange beasts had enlarged heads with very thick skulls. *Stegoceras* was probably about 6 feet long, with a domed, knobby skull. The largest of the pachycephalosaurs was called *Pachycephalosaurus*. It grew up to 26 feet long and had a huge dome of solid bone on its head.

Duckbill headgear came in many different designs. There were many types of lambeosaurs (crested duckbills), from *Corythosaurus*, with his plate-like head, to the beautifully crowned *Lambeosaurus*. Some may have had inflatable sacks on their heads to attract mates or communicate.

(Opposite) Dinosaurs had many crowns, horns and frills which may have been as colorful as tropical birds. From left to right: *Pachyrhinosaurus, Parasaurolophus, Styracosaurus* (larger than life in background), *Lambeosaurus, Corythosaurus,* and the bony-headed pachycephalosaur *Stegoceras*.

DINOSAUR SONGS

As we have seen, the duckbills were among the most well-dressed. The most spectacular one was *Parasaurolophus*. This beauty had a long, tube-shaped head. Inside were air passages that may have been used to make sounds.

Dinosaur song must have been amazing. We can tell the different kinds of birds around us by hearing their song. Dinosaurs were probably the same way. A Jurassic jungle must have been full of grunts, whines, wheezes, and bugles from these majestic animals. Some dinosaurs may have used sound as a weapon, actually causing pain to an attacker.

Says paleontologist Robert Bakker: "Lots of dinosaurs have big nostrils. These are echo chambers for making loud noises, like horses when they whinny. But some dinosaurs have small nostrils, and you say, 'How is that going to make any noise?' One of my students solved that. The bones get paper thin right below the eye—so thin they can hinge, like the reed on a huge saxophone. When the dinosaur exhaled, the thin bone vibrated. Elephants produce vibrations so deep that you can feel them. It's called infra-sound, and it will travel 10 to 20 miles. They use this sound to attract mates and to keep the family together. Most dinosaurs produced sound, and the easiest way to tell the species apart is to look for the vibrating element."

The age of dinosaurs is divided into three periods. Triassic plants *(left scene)* include ferns and horsetails along the riverbank. A palm-like cycad is on the far shore. The early dinosaur *Plateosaurus* stands in front of trees similar to today's sequoias. In the center landscape, a *Dilophosaurus* hides behind ginkgo leaves in a Jurassic jungle. Cycads are to the left. Trees at left are similar to today's Norfolk Island pines. Tree ferns grow at right. In the Cretaceous fossils *(right panel)* we find the first flowers. Here we see magnolias and flowering water lilies in a bald cypress swamp. High above is a flying *Quetzalcoatalus*.

(Inset) Ancient fossils show trees similar to these giant sequoia trees in California.

DOES THE EARTH CHANGE?

THE SCIENCE OF GEOLOGY

Where do we find fossils? In many places. They can be buried deep in the ground, in the banks of rivers, or on the sides of hills. Some fossils even end up on mountain tops. How this happens has to do with the way our planet works.

Floods are one tool God uses to change the Earth. The Bible tells of the great flood; Noah was commanded to build an ark in which he put every kind of animal. There is evidence of great flooding in many places on our planet. In 1996, there was a great flood in Iceland. This flood happened when a volcano erupted under a glacier. The melted glacier water rushed out, destroying the main highway and several bridges. Fortunately, Icelandic people are used to erupting volcanoes and melting glaciers. They were ready for the flood, and no one was killed. It is precisely this kind

of flood that preserved many of the dinosaur fossils we see today. It is clear that many floods have changed the Earth's landscapes over time. Big floods bury things quickly. Many fossils have been protected and preserved because their bodies were buried fast under mud and sand brought by floods. As Robert Bakker says, "If you want to be a good fossil, you have to be buried really fast."

Another force that changes the Earth is far more gradual. It is called **plate tectonics**. When astronauts look down from the space shuttle *Atlantis*, they can see that the edges of the continents match. The coastline of Africa fits almost perfectly against South America, and the Arabian peninsula matches up with Africa and Asia like a piece of a puzzle. In fact, Earth has been called the puzzle planet, because its continents float like puzzle pieces on a "sea" of melted rock called **magma**. These stony pieces of the plane-

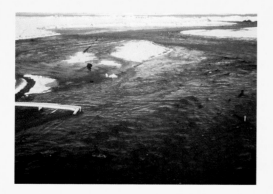

(Left) The earth has massive floods even today. In 1996, an erupting volcano melted a glacier in Iceland, triggering a huge flood which destroyed a highway and bridges. No people were killed.

(Middle) Water gushes from an Icelandic glacier after a volcano caused a huge area of the ice to melt. These icebergs are larger than houses.

(Right) The flood from this glacier broke off huge icebergs.

tary puzzle are called **tectonic plates**. Sometimes these plates bump into each other and push up mountains. Still others are pulling away from each other. In places like Iceland scientists can actually measure the ground growing apart where new ground is pushing up from underneath.

Other plates slide under each other, creating chains of volcanoes along their edges. These volcanoes erupt, bringing magma and ash from inside the Earth and spreading it across the surface. Like floods, volcanic eruptions have preserved many fossils.

Tectonic plates move about as fast as our fingernails grow. Long ago, there was an ocean in the middle of the United States, and Asia was stuck to what is now Alaska! All these moving and shaking plates led to another change in the earth. Mountains are pushed up as plates shove together. What was once on the bottom of the sea is now high in some mountains, like the Burgess Shale in the Canadian Rockies or fish fossils high in the mountains of Asia.

We see layers of rocks throughout the world. These layers started out as sand or mud. Over the years, more mud and sand settled on top, washing down from higher places. This wearing down by weather is called erosion. Just as newer cities were buried atop more ancient cities that had been covered by eroding soil, so fossils of more recent dinosaurs are buried atop those of dinosaurs that lived earlier. It is erosion that often exposes fossils that were buried deep in the ground.

Scientists also know that the climate, or weather patterns, have changed. In Bible times, there were lions and forests where deserts are now. We can also tell by fossils that the climate was different when the dinosaurs were around. Beneath the Great Plains of the United States can be found the fossils from what was once a steamy mangrove swamp. These changes are part of God's design for our dynamic world.

(Left) The layers buried deep inside the Earth are pushed up by the mountains. When weather wears the mountains away, or when we cut through them to make roadways, we see the layers. Often, this is how dinosaurs are discovered.
(Right) Where pine forests grow in the Rocky Mountains today, we find fossils of muddy lake beds and plants from mangrove swamps. This shows us that the area used to be tropical and very different from what we find now. Here we see ripples of what used to be mud and marks from leaves and twigs of swamp plants.

HOW OLD IS THE EARTH?

People have wondered how old the Earth is for a long time. The Bible says that God made the universe and everything in it "in six days," and that He rested on the seventh day. This is why we rest from work and worship God together once each week. Many Christians believe that the earth was created in six 24-hour days. In that case, the dinosaurs would probably have been around at the time that Noah was building his ark and would have been wiped out in the great flood that covered the earth.

But many of the ancient church leaders, including godly men such as Origen, Justin Martyr, and John Calvin, believed the Bible speaks of our universe as very old. They pointed out that the Hebrew word for "day" in Genesis (*yom*) can also mean a long period of time—even millions or billions of years! Christians who believe in an older Earth also point out that, according to Genesis, God continued to create new things right up until the time of people.

Genesis makes it clear that God made animals before he made us, and some of those creatures, including dinosaurs, may have been gone long before people.

Three things are important to remember: (1) Our view of the Earth must be in line with God's truth, (2) God's Creation reflects and brings glory to its maker, and (3) the age of the Earth is interesting but not as important as the Gospel message that Jesus brings to us. Time seems different to God than it does to us. Psalm 90:4 says, "For a thousand years in your sight is like a day that has just gone by. . . ."

God is pleased when we use our minds to try to figure things out, because it helps us to see how great the Creation and its Creator are. The prophet Isaiah said, "Come, let us reason together." (Isaiah 1:18) But God doesn't expect us to know everything. What's important to Him is that we know and love Him. As Jack Horner says, "Faith is about a relationship with God. How everything got here is less significant."

We know that God created everything. Christians have different opinions on God's timeline in His process of Creation. How long it took is interesting to talk about, but the most important issue of our faith is that God loves us so much that he sent His Son, Jesus, to take away our sins and give us a free, full life that will never end. This truth is clear and plain and is the very heart of our relationship with God.

> ## FUN FACTS
>
> **When did dinosaurs reach their full adult size?** Guess what? Dinosaurs never stopped growing! Mammals have a special end cap on their bones, which seals and stops growth at a certain time. But dinosaur bones don't have this feature, and they never stopped growing. Modern reptiles are the same way, so if you are planning to get a pet iguana, remember, he'll keep growing his whole life. How big is your bedroom?!

HOW SCIENTISTS ESTIMATE THE AGE OF THE EARTH

Scientists can tell how old something is by using several clues left behind in God's Creation. One of these clues is called **stratification**. As we saw in "How Fossils Are Formed," stratification is the layering of rock and soil.

When we look at the mountains we see many different colored layers of rock. The highest layers are usually the newest. When scientists dig in the Holy Land to find ancient civilizations, they know that the layers closest to the surface are the remains of the most recent towns. The deeper they dig, the more ancient things they find. Archaeologists (people who study ancient civilizations) use layers to understand what came when. Sometimes the layers get folded and moved around because of the Earth's plate tectonics, but it is still possible to tell which one goes where by comparing kinds of fossils and the order of rock layers. It takes a long time for mud and sand to turn into hard rock, and we see many thousands of rock layers in the skin of the earth, so stratification gives us the idea that the world has been around for a long time.

Another tool that scientists use is called **radiometric dating**. When God put the Earth together, there were radioactive rocks inside. These rocks are still around today, keeping the core of the Earth hot. Radioactivity in these rocks slowly fades away, changing into a different form at a steady rate. Scientists have found several elements to test the age of things. Carbon 14 changes into nitrogen at a known speed and is good for telling the age of things that are a few thousand years old. The amount of carbon 14 goes down as the age goes up. Carbon 14 doesn't work with rocks and older fossils, but other types of radioactive elements do. Rubidium (which turns into strontium) and potassium (which turns to argon) can be used as rock clocks. The ages that these elements give us do not always agree, and scientists must use many clues to figure out just how old something is. All of these tests indicate that the Earth is very old.

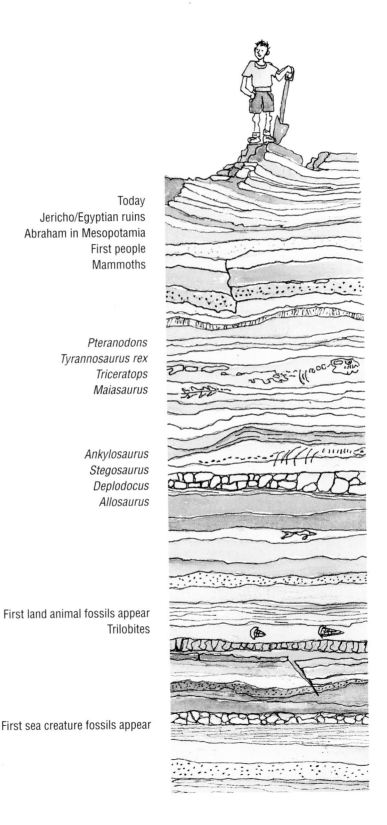

Today
Jericho/Egyptian ruins
Abraham in Mesopotamia
First people
Mammoths

Pteranodons
Tyrannosaurus rex
Triceratops
Maiasaurus

Ankylosaurus
Stegosaurus
Deplodocus
Allosaurus

First land animal fossils appear
Trilobites

First sea creature fossils appear

THE SCIENCE Of PALEONTOLOGY

OUR CHANGING VIEW Of DINOSAURS

When the first big dinosaur bones were found, people wondered how such a large creature could ever have existed. How did it hold itself up? Did it spend all of its life in lakes and rivers, letting the water hold up its gigantic body? As more bones were found, it appeared to many that the dinosaurs were like reptiles. Reptiles are cold-blooded. This means that their bodies don't make heat but remain close to the temperature around them. Reptiles get sluggish when it is cold, because their bodies cool down. Mammals and birds are warm-blooded; their bodies can make their own heat. This means that no matter what the weather is like, warm-blooded creatures remain active and alert.

For a long time, most paleontologists believed that dinosaurs were cold-blooded, lizard-like creatures that basked in the sun and could barely carry their own weight. This is how Richard Owen got the name dinosaur, or "terrible lizard." Many dinosaurs even had hips like lizards, and they are known as the **saurischians**. The saurischian dinosaurs include the theropods (meat-eaters like tyrannosaurs and raptors) and the long-necked sauropods (like *Diplodocus* and *Apatosaurus*). Even though he noticed how lizard-like some dinosaur bones were, Owen suspected that these creatures were not cold-blooded

like lizards, but "closer to warm-blooded mammals."

There were other dinosaurs that had hips like birds, and these are called the **ornithischians**. They include stegosaurs, ankylosaurs, hadrosaurs, iguanodons, and ceratopsians. Scientists began to realize that the dinosaurs had more in common with birds than just hips. Dinosaur bones also have many tiny blood vessels in them, like bird bones. In fact, dinosaur skeletons are like bird skeletons in 125 ways. Perhaps a better name for dinosaurs would have been *dinogallus*, or "terrible chicken." (But dinogallus doesn't sound as good as dinosaur, does it?) The breastbone of a dinosaur found in Italy is identical to that of a bird, but its liver, preserved in stone, seems more like a lizard's.

Another new clue is that many dinosaurs seem to have had feathers (See Some New Fossil Finds on page 11). It is possible that baby dinosaurs were covered with soft down like a baby chick, only to lose the feathers as they grew.

Were dinosaurs more like giant lizards, or were they bird-like? The mystery continues. One thing is certain: dinosaurs were agile and active, able to run and dash more like birds than reptiles.

(Right) People used to think of *Iguanodons* as heavy lizards with horns on their noses. But it turns out that the "horn" was actually a thumb attached to a mitten-like hand. Iguanodons could use their little fingers to grasp twigs and leaves to eat. They were able to stand on two feet or walk on all fours.

---

f U N   f A C T S

Where have the most dinosaur fossils been found?
Alberta, Canada

ASSEMBLY PROBLEMS

The idea of sluggish, cold-blooded dinosaurs is not the only wrong idea that early scientists had. The case of the *Iguanodon* shows us how scientists learn as more fossils are found. When *Iguanodons* were first found, they were seen as gigantic, slug-like lizards with rhinoceros horns on their noses. But scientists kept finding more horns than heads. It turned out that *Iguanodons* were graceful creatures that stood upright, unlike lizards. The mysterious extra horns were explained when complete fossils were found. The "horns" were actually sharp thumbs, probably used for digging roots and defending against predators. Museum curators had to hurry and remove the "horns" from their *Iguanodons* and glue them onto the thumbs!

As we saw with the *Iguanodons*, trying to figure out what a dinosaur looked like is tricky work. Fossils usually have parts missing, and the paleontologist must guess how the bones went together. Sometimes many bones from several different animals are found in one place, and the scientist must sort them out.

Even when a fairly whole skeleton is found, it is sometimes difficult to put the bones together right. Imagine finding the mixed-up skeleton of an anteater, giraffe, or poodle and trying to put it together, especially if you had never seen one! This is the problem which faced the explorers who came upon the bones of what they called *Brontosaurus*. In 1879, Othniel Marsh found a huge skeleton in Wyoming. Nearly all of the bones were there, but it was missing its head. Everything about the creature was thick: it had thick leg bones—bigger around than a grown man! The tail was thick. The neck was thick. It only made sense that the missing head would be thick, too. After all, big animals like rhinos and elephants have big heads, too. A fossil skull found a few miles away looked like it might belong to this kind of creature. Marsh was sure that even if the head came from a different animal, it must have been from the same *kind* of creature.

Meanwhile, near Golden, Colorado, a similar dinosaur skeleton had been found. It was named *Apatosaurus* after other dinosaurs like it that had been found earlier. It was not in very good shape, and the head was bashed in, but it was obvious that this huge creature had a tiny noggin. Says Robert Bakker, "It was like taking the head of Bambi and putting it on the neck of an elephant." No one made a connection between the two dinosaurs.

In 1899, paleontologists found the first *Diplodocus* with its long neck and narrow, tiny skull. The graceful head of *Diplodocus* had long teeth and a thin chin. Some bone experts pointed out that even though they were different in size, the *Brontosaurus* and the *Diplodocus* were the same animal. It didn't seem right that their heads were so different. But it was true: the big, boxy head of *Brontosaurus* did not belong to the more graceful *Diplodocus*. In fact, it belonged to a heavier dinosaur now known as *Camarasaurus*. True *Brontosaurus* (which are now known as *Apatosaurus*) have heavy bodies and necks like *Diplodocus*, topped with dainty heads. As more fossils are found, we have a clearer picture of what God's beautiful beasts were really like.

Scientists are still arguing about how **sauropods** (long-necked dinosaurs) walked and ate. With such long necks, scientists wonder how sauropod hearts could have been strong enough to keep blood flowing up to their heads. Some scientists have proposed that the sauropod never raised its head above its shoulders, eating like a giant vacuum, moving its long neck from side to side. Others point out that if *Diplodocus* and its cousins couldn't raise their heads to eat the tops of tall trees, there would be no reason for them to have such long necks. How these creatures moved is still a mystery.

The heavy head of *Camarasaurus (far left)* was first thought to fit on top of the strong neck of *Diplodocus (center)*. Later, scientists found out that *Diplodocus* had a delicate, horse-like head and probably held its neck close to the ground. *Camarasaurus* and other long-necks like *Mamenchisaurus (far right)* could reach up to eat the tree tops.

WORKING IN THE FIELD

The way fossils are found hasn't changed much over the years. Most fossil sites are found by accident: by farmers plowing their fields, in stone quarries, on construction sites, and by people hiking along cliffs and river bottoms where erosion takes place. So keep your eyes open! You never know when you will spot a fossil.

Early fossil finders often blew the fossils out of the ground with dynamite. But today, fossils are studied carefully before they get taken out of the ground. The paleontologist looks at the **sediment** around the fossil, and at any fossilized insects and plants to try to learn more about the life and times of the dinosaur.

The job of a paleontologist is not glamorous. Much of his or her time is spent working in very hot, flat, windy, isolated areas that are full of sagebrush and rattlesnakes. Digging starts with large picks and shovels. The last 6–12 inches of rock is removed with small awls and flat trowels. Then, slowly and patiently, the delicate work of exposing

the bones with brushes and dental tools begins. Once the fossil is out of the rock, sealing resin is often brushed on to harden the fragile fossil bones. Large bones are covered in plastic wrap, then covered with plaster, to protect them while they are transported. If you think the field work of getting the fossil out of the ground sounds tedious, try being a technician at the museum. It takes ten times as long to prepare and assemble a specimen for display as it does to dig it out of the ground.

Why do they do it? Why do paleontologists spend much of their lives in these uncomfortable and often frustrating situations? They do it for the thrill of finding buried treasure, to find out what the world was like in the past, and to see how the forces of nature caused that world to change! These things give us all perspective on modern life. Says Jack Horner, "Only by studying the past can we understand the future."

(Left) Digging dinosaur bones out of hard rock is slow, difficult work.

(Middle) Once the fossil of a bone is found, the rock around it is scraped away.

(Right) This fragile sauropod fossil has been glued in several places where it broke.

HIGH-TECH PALEONTOLOGY

Ground-penetrating **radar** has been used by archeologists to find ancient buildings underground. Stone walls have a different density than the dirt around them, and the radar can pick that up. But it isn't an easy way to pinpoint dinosaur fossils. Since fossils are nearly the same density as the stone surrounding them, the radar can't see them well. Special **Geiger counters** (instruments which measure radioactivity) can sometimes be used to spot fossils, because the concentrated minerals within the fossil are slightly more radioactive than the surrounding rock. Don't panic! The radiation in fossils is at a very low level and is not harmful at all. Once a good dig site is found, modern paleontologists use global positioning satellites to mark the coordinates of the spot so they can find it again.

Once the fossils get back to the museum all kinds of new tools can go to work on them. Scanning electron microscopes allow scientists to study the cell structure of dinosaurs in new ways. Computer programs are being developed to animate pictures of the skeletons and see how the dinosaurs may have moved. Celeste Horner, who works in the field and in the lab with her husband, Jack, is working with scientists at the University of California at Berkeley to develop a *T-rex* computer animation program that shows how the living animal may have moved.

Researchers also use computer technology to "map" dinosaur skeletons. Using a laser beam, scientists can create a detailed map of each bone on a fossil skeleton. A team at the Smithsonian Institute recently mapped the skeleton of a *Triceratops* that was beginning to fall apart. With the new map, the skeleton's precious information was saved, and the skeleton can be moved around for further study, all inside the computer, with no damage to the fragile bones!

(Left) Paleontologist Rod Scheetz of Grand Junction's Museum of Western Colorado makes a map of where the fossils lie in the ground.

(Middle) Bone fossils are wrapped in protective paper and numbered for later study. Note the giant column-shaped backbone of an apatosaur on the tailgate.

(Right) Robert Bakker

MAKIN' TRACKS: WHAT THE FOOTPRINTS TELL US

Dinosaurs have left more than bones for us to find. If the ground was just wet enough and the weather was just right, long trains of dinosaur footprints were preserved forever in what was once sand or mud. These places are called **trackways**.

Native Americans knew about dinosaur footprints. **Petroglyphs** (Indian rock-writing) are found next to several trackways. In fact, one footprint area has an Indian name meaning "Place of the bird tracks."

Dinosaur trackways have much to tell us, but sometimes we can get the wrong idea. In Paluxy, Texas, long trails of dinosaur tracks spread across the landscape in rocks called the Glen Rose Formation. Some tracks are made up of three-toed prints left by a long-necked sauropod, probably a *Pleurocoelus*. During the 1920s, people claimed that there were large footprints of a person walking with the dinosaur. This person, they believed, was wearing moccasins or soft shoes, because the toes could not be seen. For many years, people used this as evidence that humans and dinosaurs lived together. Then, in 1975, a Christian geologist named Neufeld found that the tracks started to change shape down the line. The same footprints

that looked like moccasins in one place actually turned out to be the prints of a small, three-toed dinosaur. At times the creature was walking softly, leaving kidney-shaped footprints much like a shoe. At other times it walked more flat-footed, showing the imprint of its toes.

An entire herd of dinosaurs left its mark in the Glen Rose Formation, where twenty-three giant sauropods traveled together. Tracks can tell scientists whether a dinosaur was a plant-eater taking a leisurely stroll as it munched veggies or a swift meat-eater chasing its prey. Often, the soft part of the feet can be seen, telling scientists about foot muscles and even skin.

Scientists can guess how quickly a creature was moving by the length of each step and the way the foot hit the ground. Most plant-eaters walk along at a speed just a bit faster than a person would walk. Some of these sauropods weighed as much as twenty-five cars! The meat-eaters were smaller and faster. One was estimated to be running at 26 miles per hour, nearly as fast as a galloping horse.

Trackways also tell us something about how dinosaurs walked. Some dinosaurs left no trail behind with their tails, so they must have kept their tails up in the air. This means, of course, that footprints tell tail tales!

(Left) Some footprints in the Paluxy dinosaur trackway look like human prints. But if they are followed far enough, they become more clear, and we can see they were actually left by a small theropod. *(Right)* This family of apatosaurs has left behind tracks in sand that will someday turn to stone. Often, tracks of young dinosaurs are found between the tracks of adults. Notice the small, three-toed prints of a meat-eater close to us.

EXTINCTION THEORIES

HEY! WHERE DID EVERYBODY GO?

There used to be lots of dinosaurs around. They came in all sizes. They were big and small, slow and fast. Some were probably pretty smart. Where did they all go? What caused their **extinction**—complete dying out? We already talked about the idea that the dinosaurs were wiped out in Noah's flood. Some Christians believe the layers we see in the rocks are caused by the Bible's great flood rather than years of erosion and plate tectonics. Floods caused by volcanoes often leave layers of sand and rock. The Bible says that everything that wasn't on Noah's ark was in deep water. If Noah couldn't fit those apatosaurs in beside the zebras and koalas, they'd be in trouble.

One problem with the idea that the dinosaurs died in the great flood is that no modern animals are found mixed in with dinosaurs. If they all died at the same time, why are there no iguanas beside the *Iguanodons*, no monkeys by the maiasaurs? This makes many believe that the dinosaurs were long gone by the time of Noah's flood.

Some believe that *T-rex* and his buds

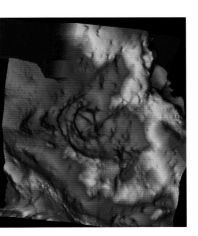

(Top) Chicxulub Crater, off the coast of Mexico. Scientists believe a big meteor smashed into the earth here, wiping out the dinosaurs.
(Bottom) Iridium is common in meteorites. The layer of white clay shown here marks the iridium layer, or "K/T boundary," found at the same depth throughout the world. No dinosaur fossils are found above this layer.

were killed off by a different natural cause: a change in the climate. As continents shift, so do the currents in our oceans and air. The Earth's climate may have gotten colder or hotter, killing off the dinosaurs.

Some scientists think an asteroid—a huge space rock—may have done the dinosaurs in. Asteroids have slammed into every surface in our solar system, and we see craters here on Earth, too. If a giant asteroid plowed into our world, it could have done more than enough damage to kill off the dinosaurs. Scientists have found a rock layer all over the world made of a rare metal called **iridium**. Iridium is found in some meteorites (small stones that fall from space). This convinces some people that the worldwide iridium layer came from a space rock. Below the layer of iridium there are the fossils of dinosaurs. Above it . . . no more dinosaurs! Perhaps an asteroid is what God used to end the time of the dinosaurs.

Robert Bakker says that most dinosaurs had already died before the iridium layer was put down. But *why* did so many die? To answer this, Bakker points to an animal disease in Africa. In the 1800s, the British army used cattle from Asia to haul cannons up the

Nile River in Africa. The Asian cows brought a disease with them called rinderpest. This sickness killed millions of African antelope. "When you mix animals together that don't belong with each other, you get hundreds and hundreds of diseases," Bakker says. At the end of the Cretaceous period, the shallow seas were draining from the North American continent, and a bridge of land had risen between Asia and the Americas. Bakker and others feel that dinosaurs were able to mix, bringing disease that wiped out entire species. Still, this doesn't explain why even dinosaurs on islands all died out.

How the dinosaurs disappeared is still a mystery. What is not a mystery is that it was part of God's plan. Whether God chose to take dinosaurs away before people—or later—is something Christians must try to figure out. We must first figure it out in light of Scripture, and where Scripture is not clear, we look to science to help fill in the holes. What do you think happened to all those beasties?

Devout people sometimes don't agree about how old the earth is. The important thing to remember is that God is in control. He is the Creator and designer of everything. Our God is great—powerful enough to make the world in six days—and vast enough to make it over billions of years.

BEHEMOTH AND LEVIATHAN: MYSTERY CREATURES OF THE BIBLE

There has been some talk over the years that **behemoths** and **leviathans** may have been dinosaurs, but most Bible scholars disagree. The *behemoth* ("great beast") is mentioned in Job 40:15-24, and Job's description of it has led Bible commentators to identify it as a gigantic species of hippopotamus. Another possibility is that it was a water buffalo. The *leviathan* ("jointed monster") is referred to in Job 41:1 and Ezekiel 29:3-5 and is thought to be a crocodile. In Psalm 104:26 the name leviathan probably represents a large species of whale.

ARE THERE DINOSAURS TODAY?

Early paleontologists had found many ancient fossils of a six-foot-long fish named **Coelacanth**. Imagine how amazed they were when, in 1938, a fisherman on the east coast of Africa brought up a live Coelacanth in his net! This bottom-dwelling fish is virtually identical to its fossil ancestors. It gives birth to live young and can swim upside down and sideways. Scientists are using submarines to learn more about this unique fellow. In 1977, a Japanese fishing boat trawling near New Zealand brought up a 4,000-pound carcass of what looked very much like a plesiosaur! But scientific analysis of the skin showed that the animal was probably a large basking shark, which easily grows that large. Basking sharks sometimes rot into a shape like a plesiosaur. Another sighting of a possible "living dinosaur" has occurred in a place called Loch Ness, a very large, deep lake in Scotland, where many people believe one or more aquatic dinosaurs live. Sightings of "The Loch Ness Monster" go back 1400 years, but aside from some blurry photographs, there is no scientific proof yet that "Nessie" really

> **fUN fACTS**
>
> **What is the most money ever paid for a fossil?** The Field Museum in Chicago purchased the fossil of Sue, the *T-rex*, for 8.4 million dollars!

exists. New species of animals are being discovered all the time, and we may discover another "living fossil" someday. Today, the closest living things to dinosaurs are the sparrows, robins, pelicans, eagles, and vultures . . . the birds!

GOD CREATES AND WE RESPOND

It appears that there once was an ocean stretching across the middle of what is now the Great Plains and Rocky Mountains. Within this sea, wonderful creatures, gigantic toothy lizards, and bizarre monsters swam. High in the sky, winged dragon-like things wheeled and soared, looking down on beasts that thundered through forests of ferns and horsetails. All of these wonders are gone now, but their fossils tell us much about what the world was like long ago. More than that, they

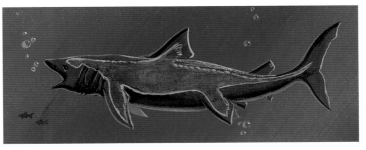
The basking shark often rots away into a shape similar to the plesiosaur.

tell us something about their Creator. God's power, majesty, mystery, and great design are painted across the stars of the sky and upon the rocks of the Earth. As the Bible tells us, "God's . . . power and divine nature have been clearly seen . . . from what has been made." (Romans 1:20).

Sometimes we look at the Creation around us, and what we see confuses us. Perhaps someone tells us that things are not really the way they appear, or scientists may say things that don't fit with what we think the Bible is telling us. What can we do?

1) First, we must realize that we might be wrong in the way we are reading our Bible or in the way we are thinking about fossils or other parts of nature. We must always look to our Bible for answers.

2) The Bible also tells us that there is "wisdom in many counselors." In other words, God has put other wise Christians in our lives so that we can find out what they think. Other Christians may know something about God's Word that we don't. It always helps to ask.

3) Pray for understanding and wisdom. In the Book of James, God reminds us that "if any of you lacks wisdom, he should ask God, who gives generously." (James 1:5).

4) Often, we don't understand something because we don't have all the facts. Look in a good dinosaur book or talk to a scientist about things that don't make sense. Often, something in science that seems to go against the Bible really makes sense when we take time to understand it.

5) As the Reverend Hitchcock said, don't be afraid of science! Science is simply our way of trying to figure out how God put the world together. Always remember that science can tell us the "how" about the world, but only God's Word can tell us the "why."

God has given us lessons in the rocks. Looking at the lifestyles of long-ago creatures gives us an idea of how much the Earth's climate has changed over time and how fragile our environment truly is. Ever since the days of Eden, God has called upon His children to care for the Earth. The dinosaurs have shown us that many kinds of God's creatures can disappear very quickly. Perhaps the best lesson we can learn from the "terrible lizards" is that God loves His Creation, and that we must care for it so that other creatures can live side by side with us. The world is wonderfully designed by a loving Creator. Let's not spoil it!

GREAT DINO VACATION SPOTS IN THE U.S.

1. **Dinosaur National Monument**
   4545 E. Highway 40, Dinosaur, Colorado
   Phone: (970)374-3000
   <u>Highlight</u>: Unique natural exhibit of 1,500 dinosaur bones forms one huge wall of the Dinosaur Quarry Visitor Center. Located in NW Colorado and NE Utah.

2. **Wyoming Dinosaur Center**
   Thermopolis, Wyoming
   Phone: 1-800-455-DINO
   <u>Highlight</u>: For a fee, you can "Dig for a Day" with scientists at a Jurassic Period quarry.

3. **Museum of the Rockies**
   Montana State University, 600 W. Kagy Blvd., Bozeman, Montana
   Phone: (406)994-2251
   <u>Highlight</u>: Fossils of a Maiasaur mother and babies

4. **Smithsonian: National Museum of Natural History**
   10th St. and Constitution Ave. N.W., Washington, D.C. Phone: (202)357-2700
   <u>Highlight</u>: Wide variety of dinosaur fossils, beautifully reconstructed

5. **American Museum of Natural History**
   Central Park West at 79th St., New York, NY Phone: (212)769-5200
   <u>Highlight</u>: The largest and most diverse display in the world: over 600 vertebrate fossils.

6. **Field Museum**
   Lakeshore Drive and Roosevelt Road, Chicago, IL (312)922-9410
   <u>Highlight</u>: See a *T-Rex* being assembled in the prep. lab for its year 2000 debut.

7. **Dinosaur Ridge,**
   Visitor Center: 16831 W. Alameda Parkway, Morrison, CO. Phone: (303)697-3466
   <u>Highlight</u>: Walk along the ancient shore of an inland sea: view over 300 dinosaur footprints.

TOP FIVE DINO WEB SITES FOR KIDS

1. ZoomSchool.com/subjects/dinosaurs
2. cotf.edu/ete/modules/msese/dinosaur.html
3. **DinoRuss' Lair:** isgs.uiuc.edu/isgsroot/dinos home.html
4. mnh.org/sue/def_life.htm
5. ucmp.berkely.edu/diapsids/dinolinks.html

GLOSSARY AND INDEX

behemoth (be-HEE-muth): A huge animal, possibly a hippopotamus, described in the Old Testament. 7, 44

camouflage (KAM-ah-flazh): The result of blending in with the natural surroundings to hide from enemies. 27

carnivore (KAR-ni-vor): A creature that eats meat. 13, 15

ceratopsian (SER-uh-TOP-see-un): Dinosaur with a frill, or collar, around the back of its head, usually having multiple horns. 18, 24, 27

Coelacanth (SEE-luh-kanth): A rare fish, thought to be extinct until a living one was found in 1938. 44

coprolite (KOP-ro-lyt): Fossilized dinosaur dung. 24

Cretaceous (kri-TAY-shus): The last time period when dinosaurs lived. 9, 28, 29

cycad (SY-cad): A seed-bearing, palm-like plant. 24, 28, 29

dinosaur: Literally means "terribly great lizard," a group of extinct creatures that share features with birds and reptiles. 7, 9, 43, 44

duckbill: A two legged plant-eating dinosaur with a broad, beak-like snout. 17, 24, 27

ecosystem (EK-o-syst-uhm): Living things and the environment they inhabit, which together make up a unit. 15

extinction (ex-TINK-shun):The death of an entire group of plants or animals. 43, 44

fossil (FAH-suhl): 1. The imprint of a living thing, turned to stone. 2. The remains of a plant or animal that has died and turned to stone. 9, 11, 12, 30, 31, 36, 38, 39

fossil field: An area where many fossils are located close together. 11, 12

Geiger counter (GY-guhr COWNT-uhr): An instrument used to measure radiation. 39

geologist (gee-AHL-uh-jist): A scientist who studies rocks and the history of the Earth. 10, 40

herbivore (HER-bi-vor): A creature that eats only plants. 17

hypothesis (hy-POTH-uh-sis): An explanation for a set of facts that can be tested to see if it is true or not. 25

iridium (i-RID-ee-um): A rare, heavy metal. 43

Jurassic (je-RASS-ik): The second geological period of the age of the dinosaurs. 9, 28, 29

leviathan (leh-VY-a-thun): A monstrous sea creature mentioned in the Old Testament, probably referring to a crocodile or a whale. 44